Felina's New Home

A Florida Panther Story

By Loran Wlodarski

Illustrated by Lew Clayton

Felina the Florida panther loved growing up in her forest home. Her mother taught her how to hunt when she was hungry, where to find cool water to drink when she was thirsty, and where to rest when the sun shone brightly.

Felina was growing, but it seemed her forest was shrinking! One day, she went to take a nap under her favorite trees, but the trees had vanished!

"Without my trees to shade me, where can I rest?" Felina mumbled.

"We wondered that too," a tiny voice said.

Felina looked around and saw a pair of red-cockaded woodpeckers staring at the barren field.

"We used to rest inside holes in these trees," the father woodpecker added.

"And that's where we would raise our family," said the mother woodpecker. "Now we don't know what to do."

"If only the trees were still here, we'd both have a place to rest," Felina said to the couple.

Felina went down a small dirt path she had traveled many times before. She couldn't believe her eyes—a road now blocked her from getting to the other side!

"With all the fast cars on this busy road, how can I get to the other side?" Felina pondered aloud.

"I wondered that too," said a sad voice.

Felina looked down and saw a gopher tortoise staring at the road.

"There's a great place for me to eat berries on the other side of this road," the gopher tortoise cried. "But the cars are going so fast that I'll never make it across. Now I don't know what to do."

"If only people slowed down to look for us or would build a safe way for wildlife to cross the road, we'd both make it to the other side." Felina said to the tortoise.

Too scared to cross the road, Felina decided to look for a safer place to rest. When she walked past some tall cabbage palms, Felina couldn't believe her eyes—noisy people were in her forest!

"Don't people know that their loud noises scare shy animals like me?" Felina muttered aloud.

"I wondered that too," a voice whispered.

Felina saw a wood stork staring at her.

"I'm looking for a quiet place where I can relax," the wood stork added. "But those people make so much noise that I'm too scared to go anywhere near them. Now I don't know what to do."

"If only the people remembered that loud noises frighten shy animals like us, we both wouldn't feel so scared," Felina said to the stork.

Felina walked toward the bay but stepped on the edge of a sharp soda can and cut her paw. Felina couldn't believe her eyes—people had left garbage everywhere!

"Don't people know that animals are hurt by their pollution?" Felina cried.

"I wondered that too," a rumbling voice said to Felina from the bay.

Felina looked in the water and saw an American crocodile surrounded by floating garbage.

"The garbage people throw away can harm all types of animals, especially if they get tangled up in it," the crocodile added. "Plus, the fish I hunt can get sick when they live in polluted water. When I eat sick fish, I feel sick too. Now I don't know what to do."

"If people would stop polluting, we'd both have cleaner homes to live in," Felina said to the crocodile.

Felina's stomach growled, so she crossed the freshwater marshes and pine flatwoods to the hunting grounds where her mother taught her how to hunt deer as a kitten. But now the fields were covered with human homes. She didn't like being near people, but Felina was hungry! Felina couldn't believe her eyes—a human was giving food to the deer she wanted to eat!

"If the people weren't feeding that deer, I wouldn't come so close to their homes. Don't they know how bad it is to feed wild animals?"

"I wondered that too," a high pitched voice said to Felina from the river.

Felina looked back towards the water and saw a Florida manatee with large scars across her back.

"When people feed animals, they may attract predators like you—if the people see you, they'll get scared and may try to hurt you," the manatee said. "Plus, other animals get hurt too. People used to give me water from their hoses or lettuce to eat, so I started coming up to them all the time. Once I came too close to a boat looking for food, and look what it did to my back. Now I don't know what to do."

"If only people would stop feeding wild animals, we'd both be safer," Felina said to the manatee.

Felina searched for food and a better place to live, but all she could find were more and more people. They seemed to be everywhere.

While looking for food one day, a man shot her with a tranquilizer!

When Felina opened her eyes, she was in a cage surrounded by many other animals. "What is this place?" Felina asked aloud.

"You're at a rescue shelter," a handsome young panther told Felina. "I'm Felix from Texas, but you can also call me a cougar, mountain lion, or puma."

"I'm Felina. Why do you have so many names, Felix?"

"Panthers are found all over the place, so people call us many different things. But you're the most rare of us all—a Florida panther."

"Why am I here, Felix?" Felina asked.

"You were very sick when they found you. Rescue people brought you here, just like the rest of us. Don't worry—these are good humans. They'll help you."

And they did. Felina's belly was full and she grew stronger and stronger every day. One day the humans gave her something that made her feel very sleepy.

Felina woke up and found herself in a new forest home. The new forest looked large and beautiful. She sniffed the air. Off in the distance she could smell deer to hunt, and even more exciting was the scent of male Florida panthers nearby. Best of all, Felina didn't smell, see, or hear any signs of humans—not even those who had brought her here.

This place was special. It was protected. There were plenty of trees to rest under, no loud noises to frighten her, no scary roads to cross, no pollution, and no people feeding wild animals. Would the humans keep this place safe for her and for the cubs she wanted to have in the future? She hoped so. At long last Felina had found her home; and she was very, very happy.

For Creative Minds

Florida Panther Fun Facts

Panther, cougar, mountain lion, and puma are all names for the same type of animal from the feline family. They are related to pet cats, as well as to tigers, cheetahs, jaguars, and bobcats. They even purr like other small cats!

Like pet cats, Florida panthers have sharp claws that can be in or out (retractable). They use these claws to grab their prey: deer, wild hogs, raccoons, rabbits, and armadillos.

If they catch a large meal, they may eat it over several days. If so, they will frequently cover it with leaves and sticks to keep it fresh and hidden from other scavengers.

Their scientific genus name, *concolor*, means "one color." That's because their fur is all one color—similar to deer, their favorite prey. Their chests are a little lighter in color.

Adult Florida panthers live by themselves and are very territorial. Each adult may use up to 200 square miles for his/her own territory. A male panther's home range overlaps with the smaller home ranges of several females.

Their habitats include both dry and wet land: cypress forests, swamps, freshwater marshes, hardwood hammocks, and woods. They prefer areas with lots of cover and lots of prey (food).

Florida Panther Life Cycle

Panthers can mate throughout the year, but most young are born in May and June.

A female usually mates for the first time when she is two years old. She will leave urine scents to let males know when she is ready. She may be heard screaming, probably because she is uncomfortable.

She will be pregnant with her kittens for about three months during which time she'll select a den in a well protected spot, usually in dense saw palmetto thickets.

The kittens are born with blue eyes and spots that help them hide while in the den. They drink their mothers' milk until they are about two months old and then they start to follow their mother out of the den (unless she is hunting).

By the time the kittens are six months old, their eyes have turned brown and their spots have faded.

At nine months, they are hunting small animals by themselves.

When they are about a year and a half, they will leave their mother and find their own territory.

Florida panthers may live to be about 12 years old, if they are lucky.

Endangered and Threatened Animals

Threatened: A species in trouble—it may become endangered if people don't help out.

Endangered: A species in a lot of trouble—it may become extinct if people don't help out.

Extinct: A species we'll never see again—extinction is forever.

The animals Felina "talks to" in this book are either endangered or threatened. Decide if the pictures shown below represent things that hurt or help animals. Answers are upside down at the bottom of the page.

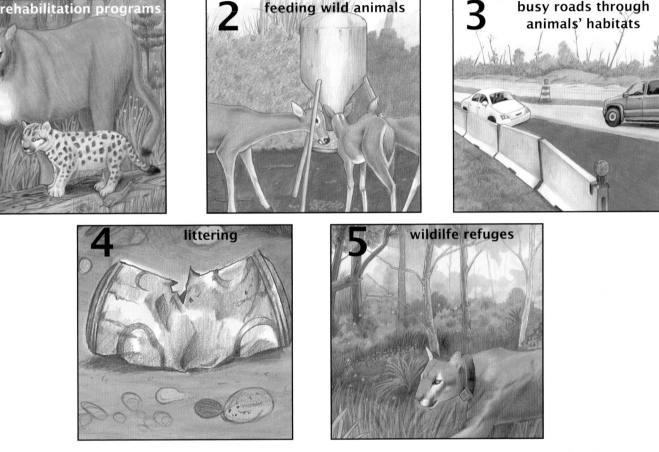

1. rehabilitation programs
2. feeding wild animals
3. busy roads through animals' habitats
4. littering
5. wildilfe refuges

1. Rehabilitation programs are designed to **help** injured animals and to hopefully return them to the wild. Sometimes injured animals cannot survive on their own, even after rehabilitation. Those animals are often sent to zoos and aquariums where they live safely.

2. Feeding wild animals can **hurt** them. Not only do they stop getting their own food, but people food can make them sick. And, because they are used to human food, they may wander into inhabited areas where they can get hurt by people or they might hurt people. Growing native plants and feeding songbirds seeds and grains that they would normally eat can **help** them. Feeding birds bread or other people food **hurts** them.

3. Busy roads going through wild animals' habitats can **hurt** the animals. They might get hit by cars or they may be unable to reach feeding or nesting areas. People have built wildlife underpasses in some areas so that wild animals can safely cross under the road.

4. Littering **hurts** animals. Some animals cut themselves on trash or can get trapped in garbage. Sometimes they eat trash (like plastic bags or balloons) thinking that it's food, and it can make them sick or even kill them.

5. Wildlife refuges **help** by providing a safe place for wild animals to live.

Match the Animal Information

Match the animal to its description, animal class and what it eats. Answers are upside down on the next page.

If a baby animal drinks milk from its mother, breathes oxygen from the air through lungs, and has hair or fur at some point in its life, it is a mammal. If an animal has feathers, it is a bird. Birds breathe oxygen from the air and hatch from eggs. If an animal breathes oxygen from the air and has scales, it is a reptile. Most reptiles hatch from eggs. All of the animals mentioned in this book have lungs to breathe oxygen from the air.

Animals that only eat meat (other animals) are called carnivores. Animals that only eat plants are called herbivores. Animals that eat both plants and meat are called omnivores.

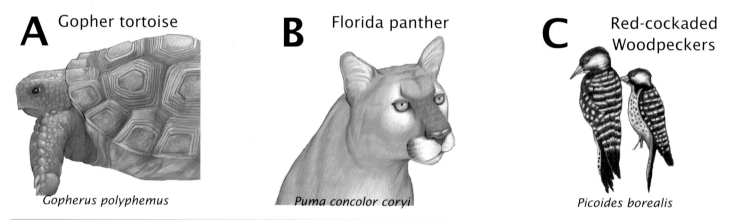

A Gopher tortoise
Gopherus polyphemus

B Florida panther
Puma concolor coryi

C Red-cockaded Woodpeckers
Picoides borealis

1 There are fewer than 100 of these animals left in the wild. North American Cougars roam the western half of the US and Canada and most of Central and South America. Separated from the cougars, this sub-species are the only cougars found east of the Mississippi and are isolated in the very southern part of Florida due to hunting and habitat loss. Several animals are hit by cars as they try to cross busy roads. People have built wildlife underpasses to help them safely cross roads. Kittens are born with spotted fur and nurse from their mothers. Like all cats, they hunt other animals for their food.

2 Their feathers are black and white but adult males have a little red spot on their heads, called a cockade. A family will peck a pine tree, usually a longleaf pine that has a fungus disease, making it easier to peck the wood. Unfortunately, the fungus needs old trees, and most of the trees were cut down by the early European settlers for farming or ship masts. It takes 100 to 150 years for new trees to grow, and seeds sprout only after a fire. Until recently, people put out the fires, making it difficult for the seedlings to sprout and grow. The animals peck holes around the nest that drip sap so that rat snakes can't reach the hatchlings. Males tend to stay with their families but females leave to start their own families. These animals eat insects, bugs, fruit and seeds.

3 These animals live in a variety of dry habitats with loose, dry, and sandy soil. Using their clawed, shovel-like front feet, they dig burrows averaging 4.5 meters (14.8 feet) in length and 2 meters (6.6 feet) in depth. This type of turtle is also called an "apex species," because many other animals or plants in their ecosystem depend on them to survive. Over 300 different types of animals rely on the turtle's burrow for their home—either while the animal lives there or after it is abandoned. Females lay eggs in the late spring to early summer and the hatchlings will spend the following winter in or around the mother's burrow. These animals eat low-growing grasses, legumes, and fruit.